CONSTITUE

WICK POETRY FIRST BOOK SERIES
Maggie Anderson, Editor

Constituents of Matter

Poems by

~~Anna Leahy~~

Anna Leahy

11/15/08

To Hadara—

Here's to the edge
     where we must dwell—
and to the poems we write there.
Best to you in all endeavors. I'm
     happy to have met you.

The Kent State University Press

Kent, Ohio

© 2007 by Anna Leahy
Library of Congress Catalog Card Number 2007021835
ISBN: 978-0-87338-925-9

Manufactured in the United States of America

Cover artwork:
In Search of Meaning #1.
An Art and Science Collaboration by Lylie Fisher.
www.lyliefisher.com

11   10   09   08   07   5   4   3   2   1

The Wick Poetry Series is sponsored in part by the Stan and Tom Wick
Poetry Center at Kent State University.

Library of Congress Cataloging-in-Publication Data

Leahy, Anna, 1965–
    Constituents of matter : poems / by Anna Leahy.
        p. cm. — (Wick poetry first book series ; no. 13)
    ISBN 978-0-87338-925-9 (pbk. : alk. paper) ∞
    I. Title.
    PS3612.E214C66 2007
    811'.6—dc22

                                    2007021835

British Library Cataloging-in-Publication data are available.

in memory of my father
Andrew J. Leahy (1933–1986)

CONTENTS

ACKNOWLEDGMENTS

Thanks to Finishing Line Press for publishing *Turns about a Point* (2006) in which the following poems appeared, sometimes in different versions:

"Moments, Causes"

"A Theory of Formation"

"Starstruck"

"A Theory of Making"

"A Fascination: The College Park Airshow, 1992"

"Collaboration, from the Latin *to slip together*"

"Recurring Dream (5)" (as "Recurring Dream")

"The Stars Don't Dance"

Thanks also to Sow's Ear Poetry Press for publishing *Hagioscope* (2000) in which "Recurring Dream (3)" appeared in a slightly different version.

I am grateful to the editors of the following literary journals and the Woman Made Gallery's calendar in which versions of my poems have appeared:

Alaska Quarterly Review: "Regalia, from the Latin *worthy of a king*" (as "At My Father's Funeral")

Connecticut Review: "Midnight Swim"

Her Mark Calendar 2001: "The Properties of Light and Villanelles" (as "Saint Lucy")

The Journal: "Moose, Looking" (as "Moose in Vermont")

Lake Effect: "Theories of Handwriting"

Nimrod: "The Many Worlds Experiment"

Phoebe: "Gestures of Flight" (as "Gestures")

River Oak Review: "A Fascination: The College Park Airshow, 1992" (as "The College Park Airshow, 1992," and nominated for a Pushcart Prize)

Spoon River Poetry Review: "Hiroshima's Secrets"

Thanks to Alberto Ríos for his generous reading and to all at the Wick Poetry Center and the Kent State University Press, especially Maggie Anderson and Mary Young.

I am grateful also for support from the Vermont Studio Center and to supportive academic colleagues along the way, among them Lisa Long and Debora Rindge. Thanks also to Steve Killings for advice on Latin.

I appreciate the numerous individuals who offered encouragement, research information, and suggestions. Among them are my mother Mary Lee, my sister Brigid, my aunt Maggie, and friends Mary Cantrell, Nancy Kuhl, Audrey Petty, and Natania Rosenfeld.

I am especially appreciative of Douglas R. Dechow, whose affection, steady support, and intellectual provocation helped shape this book.

In one of the poems crafting this compelling collection, a father gives the speaker's sister a quarter, a mechanism for calling should she run into trouble on her first car date. It is a simple talisman, of both science and desire, a quarter with a singular intention. The speaker ends this poem by saying, "This I appreciate: a beguile my father shares / with my sister, with purpose, and on each other's behalf." This act is an extension of all the richness that thrives, however quietly, in these poems—simplicity, complexity, love, science, humor, fear—and all of it so often all at once.

The poems in Anna Leahy's *Constituents of Matter* are poems of tender perplexity, confident of voice on first reading but easily enough understood more candidly as what they really are: brave declarations. They reconcile *tough* and *vulnerable* all the way through the book, to profound, often memorable effect. And in that process, they do not let go of our hands. We are in this together.

There are people in these poems like we are people, people guided by things—they think it's themselves, but so much more presents itself every step of the way. And the guide is not simply what we know, but what we don't know, as well, and what we remember and what we imagine, so that the moment is easily asserted, a few poems later, as being "full of absent parts."

When science meets and moves in with a real life lived, compelling and even grand things start to happen, but understandable best as everyday circumstance rather than textbook examples. Anna Leahy's poems offer us a building sensibility that both thinks and feels, not one at the expense of the other. That gives them complexity by dimension, rather than by the simple addition of more details, these poems plumbing high and low as much as near and nearer. The experiences recounted are rendered as nonstop intellectually engaging ideas, but with stories tethered to those ideas, good stories, hard sometimes but always loving, with high seriousness and humor both, and our greater shared humanity running underneath it all.

Found in these pages as well is simple profundity, desire unmitigated, the things we wish for each other, the science of absolutes so easy to understand, and so devastating: these poems put complex moments in such a straightforward context that we grasp not simply the words but the full feeling as something we have felt in some kind of similar vocabulary: "God is the luck my family wanted / me to have. . . ." That God and luck might be so easily associated speaks to the human heart, our deepest wish to protect someone else and even ourselves.

The desires and comparisons offered throughout are not to shock, but to grasp, to understand something in the moment from which we draw feeling: "Our smiles were upside down to each other. He could not swim." Looking at a dying father lying in a bed, the reporting of two smiles leads us with its simplicity to understand very quickly something of the universe in that instant. One thing might so easily be confused with the other, but the difference is everything. A subsequent poem suggests, similarly, the striking confusion from a distance between someone stamping spiders and that same body motion seeming so similar to happiness and exuberance.

Near the end of *Constituents of Matter,* one of the almost casual observations lithely embedded in a poem speaks the whole book: "No one knew / their words had left the earth, had made language a flight." No one knew, until now.

I don't know what makes us open books, what makes us want to stay with them, what makes us find their ends, other than the idea that good writing leads us. This book led me, and I was glad. Its science was also its heart, a question mark twice over, whose answer was not an answer but time well spent along the path.

I. UP/DOWN

MOMENTS, CAUSES

*Modern man has used cause-and-effect as ancient man used
the gods to give order to the Universe. This is not because it was
the truest system, but because it was the most convenient.*
—HENRI POINCARÉ

Moments arrive like mothers, inevitably
   seamless and charming. History
      is thunder following lightning,

two moments from one cause,
   the seen and then the heard.
      Even the blind, when a light is shone

from a heatless, strangered distance,
   know the silent light's direction:
      up or down—there, there, now.

But wait! When out of time, out of place,
   one particular thing becomes another
      unseemingly: the overlapping

like tops and bottoms of waves that is metaphor.
   What are mothers for,
      if not to teach us to swim

by showing us the motions of arms and legs
   and planets, of flavors and colors, fathers and lovers,
      and holding our young bellies

until we put our faces in the water
   with our breaths held?
      Water, then, is breathtaking,

and we float, suspended
   in we know not what
      until, knowing, we glide.

Remember the writing tablet,
each line wide with its dashed center.
Remember the cursive alphabet
circling the classroom
above the blackboard where everyone
could see it, white letters on green,
and the word *cursive* itself
such decadence at seven years old.
Remember the patience,
moving pencil to top of line,
the curve, the half-heights
of lower case, repetition.
Remember how hard
the *G,* the *D,* how easy the *I.*
The balance, remember the balance
above and below, up and down,
the importance of length,
and the looping, so unnecessary
but lovely and full
and correct.

~

In Latin class, who am I
to tell the difference
between accent marks, to know
which are simply innate sound,
to mark other syllables with import
like stamens
dashing visibly from orchids?
I sit at a table alone in a next-door room
with a nosebleed, small clots in my throat
let loose, red-soaked tissues,
a bouquet in my hands

while the rest of class conjugates
unwildly and without
the inflection I think possible
if markings mean anything.

~

I cannot tell one nun's handwriting
from another's, nor from my grandmother's.
All the same, all perfect.
I guess, though, at their years,
the now-thoughtless focus.

~

In written Mandarin, *autumn* is *crops on fire.*
The language is tenseless, numberless,
and, therefore, open to suggestion,
suggestive. In Latin, *suggerere, to carry under*
so that metaphor is what underlies,
a tunnel burrowed beneath one thing
to another, the meaning carried through.
Juxtaposition requires no tunnel.
And Mandarin's *sorrow*
is *autumn on the heart.*

~

I was reprimanded for printing,
told that I was not revealing
what God had made me.
Cursive is from *course,* as in flowing,
as in blood coursing through your veins
like sepals and petals loosening

to bloom, taking shape.
How perceptive of someone to recognize
that handwriting is self-expression,
how bold of some nun to say this
to my face.

~

The thumb down the jaw
like a bonnet string for *female*
and then the hands held out
to hold the imagined baby
for *mother*. And *male*
is the fingers coming together
with the thumb as if
grasping the brim of a hat.
The father I know
is the thumb tapping temple,
fingers wiggling.
The question is merely a stroke
with the right index finger
across the left digits
or the index finger circling
in front of the lips
as if applying lipstick
on a round mouth.
And the answer,
three extended fingers
moved in an arc
across the heart,
shoulder to shoulder: *we.*

~

A friend confides in me
that the Chinese character for *factory*
is now just a roof without machinery,

that *immense* is full of emptiness too,
that the written language now confuses
after, behind, and *queen.*
In writing, nothing is unintentional,
not even confusion,
and revolution can be simplification.

~

Remember handwritten stories
with crayon drawings. Remember
doodles in the margins during class,
the flowers' five-petal corollas
and curved petioles, pointed leaves
and the words on the page, lighter,
less planned
but wholly ordered by something
beyond hand and pen,
the words unthinking
next to the bursting, marginal ivy.
Remember a grandfather's recipes,
a list of ingredients
without instructions
on large index cards: French toast
with thick bread left out overnight to dry,
salad dressing with lemon juice
squeezed fresh into the oil,
chicken salad with capers.
Remember his hands, holding
a fork, reading, and, after, a cigarette
drifting curlicues.

~

The handwritten gives way,
eventually relinquishes fingers to keyboard,
as if to first frost.

Still, I remember and begin with pen
and ruled paper and their ability
to strike through
and allow me to still see *it*
there under the dark line
of my new intentions.
Joy lies in the missed crossing
of a *t,* the dot of an *i* lingering
down the line.
Each letter moves
into the next and the next
as with lilacs, lilies of the valley,
and, sometimes, an iris
appearing out of nowhere.

A THEORY OF PALMS

On New Year's Eve, I spin the fringe
   of my skirt between thumb and forefinger
      like a bet or a bribe.

   What makes people want to be told
   things about themselves they already know?
The left hand is destiny, a fixed form,

the right is the willfulness you're humming,
   the difference between them like the turn
      of a sonnet: *ah-hah.*

   A crooked finger means just that.
   What's in my voice that someone pulls away and another asks for more,
both slipping me a buck for beauty or truth?

The thumb's a metrical digit—that's what it reveals.
   The syntax of its flexibility
      is uncanny: *you're a tight-ass, you're a cheapskate,*

      you're a giver, a pushover, a doormat.
   Am I no longer guessing if I hit a nerve?
Do you long for the lucky handcuffs,

wonder whether you can speak with animals?
   Let me pinch you.
      Marriage—its length, its lilt—is simple to gauge,

      children, to count as notches like paper cuts.
   Divorce looks like enjambment, lines broken in midst
but I need only look at the cohorts, the glass, the time

the hand pulls away. The magic *M:*
   money or marriage. Which do you want?
      I am ringed by melancholy, and tomorrow's next year.

Clearly, I've willed myself barren,
   despite a strong girdle of Venus
and belief in hypergraphia, hands fingering words uncontrollably.

My thumb's chained. I'm steadfast.
   What can a poet do with such practical phalanges?
      The lines re-etched, the left and right hands move toward matching.

MIDNIGHT SWIM

At seven years old, I should have been in bed.
Instead, the suits, the beach, the August moon,

The air cooled as if by magic—the night itself
A bewitched pleasure I don't speak of.

Pebbles—the solid things in this world—
Shift, footed by my enchanted tiptoes

Like starlight striking. To keep my head above water,
I unhitch my arms. They float.

My thighs rise in the murky lake.
All I know of my body I learn at this moment

Of unwilling my small self.
My sister's screech travels across the lake.

We hear it leaving us. We hear midnight
Taking it in, just as midnight takes light

Into its gargantuan self. We hear mosquitoes
Around our heads waiting for us

To offer our skin. I imagine myself
A fish, a scuba diver, a boat, here with translucent ferns

Against legs, twigs, and the shadow of our peninsula
In the shadow of our sky. I find a cold spot,

Float half in it, half out, thinking two thoughts at once.
Like lake and sky. I believe I can do anything and will.

I believe my parents bring me to lakes
So that I can disappear into them, into the grace

Of liquid, and come back knowing who I am
And why. I come back each time needing more

From this moment, any moment, more than a lifetime
Can possibly offer me: an unbelieving, unwilling girl

In the world's midnight at my age of reason.
I leave sleepy and slaked, listening to our lake

As we drift toward an obsequious daylight,
Toward our buoyant waking.

MOOSE, LOOKING

It's the jowls, really,
and the water dropping from them,
the beautiful unslurping
just next to the car, idling.
And the brown
of its coat, molting,
and of its round eye
dark enough to contain the field, the ditch,
and the moose's large life.
And my life even.
The scene is unstartling
for the moose, and somehow
for me too
because of the jowls, the eye, and the slow
rise of its forequarters
from its hind
like the landscape itself
ambling up to me
for a long drink
I can never really have.

THE PROPERTIES OF LIGHT AND VILLANELLES

after Saint Lucy

A saint must be both particle and wave.
Beyond light is immeasurable mass.
The spaces between crests are what eyes crave.

One's good sight should not be scorched at the stake
Or left at local brothels, loose and fast.
A saint must be particular. The wave-

Length of red is long. Particles have
Shape and sort. Retinas gaze the unvast
Distance between crests. How eyes must crave

When pulled from a face to sit on a plate.
What if her eyes see only peaks that pass?
A saint must be all particle, all wave:

Matter and motion, part and parcel. Grave
Rods mistake a finger's pressure for blasts
Of space not mass. And crests can make eyes crave.

Lucy exchanges her eyes for favors
And holds her eyes so she can always cast.
A saint must be both particle and wave:
Between the crests, it is space her eyes crave.

It is the light she longs to find,
When she delights in learning more.
Her world is learning: it defines
The destiny she's reaching for.
　—MARIE CURIE

I.

At nineteen, Albert Einstein picks up an apple and an orange in the market. Today, this is two, but there are many ways of counting, and, of course, he knows apples and oranges should never be compared. He wants both but does not buy either. His wife may not be strong enough to endure this kind of resistance.

II.

At the evening garden party, Marie Curie lifts a glowing test tube out of her pocket to show her colleagues what she has discovered. Everyone stares at her husband's hands in the strange light. Later, she smooths ointment on his hands and bandages them. She knows it is too late for anything more.

III.

Werner Heisenberg hikes all day at a steady pace to clear his head. It is too cold to swim, even for him. When he gets home, he remembers only one particular tree, the way its limbs arched as if growing. Or was that his wife lifting herself up from her garden, waving to him even? Or, he thinks, that may have been a different hike altogether.

IV.

Enrico Fermi listens to Neils Bohr carefully. Who wouldn't? He knows that later he will not remember if he was surprised at the question. He straightens his jacket as if that is answer enough. To accept a Nobel Prize is rarely such a difficult choice. His wife will be pleased, he will have to write a speech, and they will leave Italy.

V.

Just as the water begins to boil, Richard Feynman and his colleague realize that spaghetti, when snapped, breaks into three pieces. Always. They break all the spaghetti they have. He is sure there is a great theory involved. His first wife has been dead many years, and he misses their dinners. He knows he will be dead soon, too.

The ball in the air, a real ball,
the hand having tossed it,
the child where he knows
he shouldn't be.
His mother would reprimand him
if only she knew also.

The groceries, the arms carrying them,
the money in her pocket
held back from her husband
who is hungry for her.

The bell on the bicycle,
under the thumb.
Feet, pedals, two wheels,
all spinning together.
Momentum, inertia,
the tire's track unfurling.

The President understands
infamy as two-way street: action,
equal and opposite reaction.
The Emperor counts too.

The woman in the kitchen,
the sink's steam rising.
The baby caught
between the inhalation and exhalation
of unbridled crying.
The knife in the butcher's hands,
the flesh unflinching.
Then, an elegant pause.

Not the bomb dropping
but the plane lifting—and light.

THE BIOLOGIST'S FALL

after W. G., Susan's father

Your fall on the icy driveway is evidence
    of the body's willingness to be

surprised into the air, let go. The impact
    locks your lungs for a few seconds

like childhood blows. On the ground,
    you think you should have worn

better shoes, maybe boots, not shoveled so well,
    should have invested in seed or salt.

After just two or three minutes, you begin
    to wonder if you will ever get up.

You think of Newton, Skinner, bacon and eggs.
    Perhaps your wife will run across you

on her way to the mailbox, the trip
    you have failed to complete.

The silence of cold gives you welcome
    ear aches, a focus and brilliance.

This fall is the most comfort
    the world has to offer now:

its demand you stay put. You hope
    the neighbors do not see you there.

Who would have thought the shoulder
    you have used so long

could shatter so easily, become
    so quickly unfamiliar and burdensome?

You have been disappointed
    by your naïve belief in yourself.

Then, as often happens in the cold,
    you have to piss and this

is the only reason you find to want
    to get up, but you wait

for the urge to pass. Were there seed,
    you might attract birds;

were there salt, you might taste
    where you've fallen, tears and home.

GESTURES OF FLIGHT

for my godmother

My grandfather announced he would die
within twenty-four hours as if it were

an estimated time of arrival taking wind
speed into account. Then, I know, you watched

him starve for almost a month, always trying
to right himself, wanting to be left

alone. When he died,
you said that if there had been a gun,

you would have shot him,
watched his frame pitch,

and that's what he would have wanted,
his body shrinking in upon itself to jettison

its cargo and weight, expelling
blood, water, shit, skin, breath, and you

cleaning him again.
You said there would be no visitation,

no funeral, no place
for people to come who had not come

already. But you changed your mind,
picked out a sleek metal casket,

called the priest, chose the readings,
the songs, all traditional hymns that voices

remember from repetition.
Your lover stood—we all saw—

alone in the back where
your mother would not look, your mother

shook her finger
at the casket, a large reprimand

in a small gesture, the language
of an old woman's hands in the air

with little left to say—
and you stood tall in your navy blue suit

singing *Onward Christian Soldiers*
like a flight attendant ready for takeoff, pointing

out emergency exits over wings
with arcs of arms and fingers,

dabbing eyes with white tissue,
oxygen masks dropping down,

bowing your head for the blessing,
placing the mask over your face and pulling

the straps tight, calmly
stating: buckle up, buck up, buckle under,

insert metal into clasp, lift
clasp to release.

A GAME THEORY

We all wish our own
lungs could hold more mystery
     "House of Cards," Mary Swander

If I had a poker face, what would the world offer?
Decisions, like lilacs, are my weakness,
lovely from a distance before the scent takes
my breath away. Ante up, draw or stand, raise, call,
somehow figure the greatest good.
My grandmother: *breast your cards, pinch back*
first buds.

God is the luck my family wanted
me to have, the whisper-mystery, the word-wisdom
to explain the pistil-stamen, Midwestern life-landscape
as if they could convince me
that every unfamiliar field were alfalfa.
My great-aunt: *I'll stake you.*

When I was young, I told my mother
all young cows shed their hair and become black
like their mothers. She should have known
something about breeding, more than
wishful thinking.
When I was young, I told my friend at camp
she could get rabies from mouse-nibbled licorice.
She was maturing before
my homesick, sneak-peek, solitaire eyes.

Nothing kept me from stomping off from the felted table,
from bursting, blooming
with anger over my own misplay.
My grandfather: *a card laid is a card played.*
My mother: *life isn't fair.*
They wanted me to have a prayer in this world.

No odds given on menu items, hair color, late-buried bulbs.
It's the decisions without risk that lose
their pollen easily, pinochle-sweetly.
My godmother: *read them and weep.*
Without *the* thing, there is everything,
useless three-card straights, my urge to draw, a gasp,
my fingers fanning, the wild card in someone else's garden
without me knowing it, doubtless.

If my prayer is well planted, well played, somehow unselfish,
what will I win? What will I get this time?

CONSTITUENTS OF MATTER

on visits to the Museum of Science and Industry, Chicago, Illinois

The heart was huge and red with a recorded
thump-thump inside. I put my hand against
a blue artery: it fit perfectly.
I could be inside myself,
hold on to something important.

~

The positive and the neutral: just gossip between them.
Electrons: uncareful orbits.
Molecules like polystyrene balls hooked together
with toothpicks—lopsided Christmas ornaments
in my sister's kindergarten hands.
With electrons and siblings, warmth creates panic.

~

A twisted ladder of answers or promises,
each rung a secret or a hope:
my lover's bald head, his grandfather's bald head,
my father's hands becoming
my hands, my mother's twisting foot bones,
her need to look at babies' feet.
In Dixon, Illinois, my great-
grandfather fell from a ladder, a weak rung
or a heart attack, died right there,
the ladder still leaning against the barn, the cows
waiting for milking.

~

The difference between weight and mass is gravity:
mass measures only what is there—the solid.
Gravity has no place in perfection,

like a prayer from an atheist echoing out of earshot,
like longing that is grief, that unmattering pull.
Electrons, too, can be ignored—
out of sight, out of mind.
What is perfect is not always worth considering.

~

Each name had its number on the shiny chart
pulled down from the tube at the front
of the classroom. Hydrogen, one.
Uranium, uranium, you rain on him.
The chart looked
like a calendar of too many days,
each element a different result
of the fusion of long-ago stars.

~

The quark is named for Joyce not cheese,
which is not really the moon's matter either.
A fraction is like a slice of the wheel, though,
or the Host broken, dropped into wine,
a third, maybe two-thirds, hard to tell
generation to generation,
some too quick, flavored, and colorful.

~

One scientist asks another,
If you are traveling in a car
in the dark at the speed of light
and you turn the headlights on,
do you see anything?

~

The difference between
nature's forces is
the coming and going of solid things,
between the body
twirling and the schoolbag spinning
around it, between
my spinning waist and the edge of my plaid skirt lifting,
between gathering
and pulling away.

~

Molecules: valences—
indistinguishable like families
sharing rooms in the house
and, down the hall, the sound of my father,
retching. Premises:
the weft and warp of things,
threads in the fabric, filaments in the thread,
the spin and twist impossible to differentiate
from the fiber itself, its color and heft.

~

Our sun is the solar system's nucleus,
the planets, its big electrons.
My bright globe—my father's gift to me—
put names to places, traced boundaries,
put me in my place in this world.

~

My adopted cousin had a model of motion
made of silver balls strung next to each other

in a small frame: Newton's cradle.
Draw
the last collision ball up, let it swing. It clicks
against the motionless row, transfers
its energy
to the other end, and makes the opposite ball
leap up.
The clicking of one and then the other,
the conservation of momentum
while devilish
friction slows them. My cousin died,
his factual mother and father each having given
a recessive gene that
makes the skin taste like salt.

~

The Earth tips on an axis like a heeling ship.
The mast against dusk, the bow turns home.

~

Behind glass plates, actual fetuses
preserved and positioned in cross-sectioned,
pinkish, plastic uteruses.
All the fetuses, their real flesh,
the same color.
Each fetus, distinct and still,
together, a mock-up of growth.
My mother tried to hurry me to hatching chicks,
but I kept looking, noting the order,
one after the other.
I retraced my steps to the first, the speck I doubted.
Either/or: the choice of what to see most truthfully,

time or space?
At the end, the testament of donation of tissue
and probability of natural causes.

~

Uranium, like memory, has a long half-life.
Beyond this: a few split-split-seconds
of reactive, salty existence, a place at the table,
men claiming *my element's heavier than yours.*

~

Doctors called my father's small tumors *masses*
as if isolated from gravity by flesh,
as if their slightness was all that elemental stability
had left for him, *masses*
as if dressed in fancy vestments and singing weightless
hymns to the surgeons' knives.

~

The Earth's orbit slows, is slowest in April,
steals split-seconds from days in August.
No one notices its eccentricity. No one sees
that our round planet bulges at its hot center.
Venus orbits like Earth, like love, counterclockwise
but, unlike Earth, in a near-perfect circle
and spinning backwards slowly, moonlessly:
two long, long days like a deathwatch.

~

Our moon's tail is faintly salty and orange.

~

Ontogeny recapitulates phylogeny: the fetuses
are a slide show of evolution, a crazy summary.
Recognize the tadpole, the monkey.
The second embryo has gill-slits,
the fourth is still attached
to a uterus; the sixth, in its gauzy amniotic sac;
the ninth, ectopic. The thirty-eighth
fetus looks like an old man, has tired creases
under his closed eyes, wrinkles in his ecru
forehead, his arms laden with skin. Each
is a bigger version of the one before, an illusion
of singular progress created by continuity of position.
All forty fetuses have been on display
here in their lighted boxes
for more than sixty years,
seven years longer than my father lived.

~

Two photographs: each a composite face,
a layering of many negatives into a single print,
a man and a woman. Typical:
the actual overlaid to make the average,
to see common features emerge,
to be everyone and no one at the same time.
It's all happenstance of light, of particle and wave
against film and then paper, and later against my retina:
just a long whisper between acquaintances.

~

Memory, like light, is matter and movement—
what travels slower than light
can never travel faster than light,
what travels faster than light can never be

proved to exist at all.
Light, like memory, is our world's border,
the edge where we must dwell.

II. CHARM/STRANGE

A THEORY OF FORMATION

They, too, labor,
And if we envy them we should remember
How brief their stay in the ether is.
     "CUMULUS," PHILLIS LEVIN

Life's the accumulation: the drive
I remember, the sky, the explanation
Of cloud formation I gave you.

Heaping and height, I ranted
With the belief that it matters
To those of us on Earth

Letting *nimbus*
Roll off our tongues
Into the spacious station wagon.

How many hours did you let me
Waste? How could I have known
To envy

Then? I find shapes in those moments
Only now, their brevity lingering
Long enough to miss

And shift. There would be no test,
Nothing beyond my mouthing
The words to you: *alto, stratus.*

The sky curtained God's eyes,
Hid us together, father and daughter,
So that I could explain the universe

And convince you to believe in me.
That's what I have, what suffices:
My trust that you trusted.

The display, now gone but then: a monk
with a tonsure circling his head,
at a desk and bent over a manuscript,
his stylus resting mid-word.
My father, now gone but then, in a too-loud voice:
and this is why the Catholic Bible is wrong.
Heads turn, of course, and he goes on:
The Church kept this monk and others like him
in small cells, gave them little to eat,
day-old bread mostly and grooo-el—
he draws out the syllables in a big frown
as if tasting the mess himself and drooling—
Imagine a week
with little sleep, a few hours a night
on uncomfortable cots of stiff straw.
Look at his clouded eyes.
A small crowd has gathered. My father gestures
with a wide arc of his arm toward the wax display.
Often they could not sleep at all, kept at their desks,
kept awake by wearing hair shirts,
their sandaled feet cold on the—he pauses—*drafty floor.*
Look at this monk.
His hand is cramped, stiff from the unrelenting task.
Someone gasps. It is true—they all see it now.
No longer can anyone there believe
that labor is love, nor translation, joy.
And yet, and then: *The only way*
the monks could take their revenge
was to—yes—*to change just a word, here and there.*
The powerless must always seek power,
even if one word at a time,
and this is why the Bible is wrong.
A man raises his hand, says, *I have a question.*
My father smiles.

PHOTOGRAPHER, FROM THE GREEK *ONE WHO DRAWS LIGHT*

In photographs at two and seven years old,
I hold one hand to my forehead to shade my eyes
and the other holds a finger to the sky
to point out something I've seen
or want to have seen, something moving.
I remember the family on vacation,
my father extending the tripod, setting the timer,
rushing to us, to the edge of some vista,
sweeping his hair from his forehead
just before the click that captured us there.
My mother held us steady just long enough.
My sister loved any camera, leaned into the lens,
cocked her head, and smiled to make round cheeks,
but I posed only for my father-photographer.

When I was four, he tucked my pants
into my striped socks—*have I ever or always
chosen*—and told me to look
serious like a palace guard
on the white steps of our white house with its red trim.
Later, I thought he thought I looked silly,
but now I think he didn't see
the chocolate around my mouth, my tousled hair.
He saw my brown leather shoes, my Peter Pan collar,
and my stern countenance, my whole small self
in his shadow. Irony is a kind of beauty.
I could be whatever we encompassed,
at least for a moment on those steps,
both of us scowling in jest to each other.

At twelve, he taught me the light meter, how to hold it
in my left hand, point it at my subject,
make decisions based on brightness, distance, and speed.
Later, I found his Voightlander camera in his closet,

held its base in my left palm, braced
my elbow against my ribs, cupped the lens lightly between
thumb and forefinger for adjustments.
I photographed people in black and white,
full of contrast that is easily confused with character.
I never considered that, after so much use, his and mine,
the internal parts would eventually stick, stop cold,
and could not be replaced
until I find a matching model intact
and swap its parts for the ones I need.

PECUNIARY, FROM THE LATIN *MONEY*

My sister's date shows up before she is ready.
It is the early 80s so it takes blow-dryers,
curling irons, and hairspray, that invisible net.
I have unwelcome wings and a perm

that I twirl around my fingers to Air Supply or AC/DC.
My father asks the boy, who fidgets with his car keys,
his intentions. He doesn't know
what my father is talking about.

This is my sister's first car date, the first time
any boy has come out to the house
instead of my father driving her into town
to meet a boy at Pizza Hut, where they play Galaga

and eat sausage and cheese pizza from a greasy pan.
Tonight, the drive-in, though my father doesn't know it
and wouldn't know *Pink Floyd: The Wall* if she said it.
My sister walks into the living room

in her synthetic purple dress and wooden wedges.
My father pulls a quarter from his pants pocket.
My sister and I have done laundry since we were
ten and twelve years old. The rule of the house

is that money left in the laundry is ours.
My father often left change in his pockets,
perhaps, I now want to think, on purpose.
Once, during my sister's laundry week,

he left twenties direct from the bank in a shirt pocket.
She returned them when she found the third and fourth.
I was a skimmer, taking quarters from the big coffee can
in my father's closet, taking more than I deserved.

Hold out your hand, he says. She smiles.
He places the quarter in her palm,
wraps her fingers back around it,
holds her hand in his. They like drama.

If this boy causes any trouble,
you call me. I'll come get you.
She laughs, rolls her eyes, places the quarter in her shoe.
The boy doesn't see the humor, which undoes him.

This I appreciate: the beguile my father shared
with my sister, with purpose, and on each other's behalf.

REVISION, FROM THE LATIN *TO SEE AGAIN*

We ate smoked salmon and brown bread
formed for us by a distant relative's ruddy hands,
we tasted the salt from the sea

on our happy tongues and felt wool's roughness on our skin,
we, silent, looked over the Book of Kells
with its elegant swirls of belief and wanting,

its way of making a word a painting, a painting holy—
if I had known then,
would I have taken you up into the mountains

above Dundalk where our ancestors are buried,
where the Conlins had lost
their teeth and drank poteen from shot glasses,

where Sister Kevin still raised a fist at slow British gunboats
in an insignificant blue river—
if I had known, would I have laid you in the grass

where the sheep could graze around your body
and I could tie strips of your clothing to the branches
dipping over a stream that runs with the blood

of a saint's self-plucked eyes,
where you could look up into the moving clouds,
imagine they are not just distant dark shapes

but the brushstrokes and penstrokes of monks and visionaries:
you would feel sick only because you were spinning
with the earth pinned to your back.

RECURRING DREAM (1)

A headache grows a ruby beneath my tongue. I pull it out like a first tooth for my father to give my mother in a ring. He swallows it. I can't stop him. It spills splendid red tumors into him. They stick to his stomach, his spleen. His belly swells. When the doctors open him up, they poke the rubies and find unexpected blood. The doctors' clamps and knives are dosimeters measuring their exposure to his uranium organs. Their gloves are lead. Over the incision, they discuss tactical bombs and carcinoma of unknown origin like priests saying mass absentmindedly. He winks at me—his mouth overflowing with rubies I must reclaim—and whispers, *we live bejeweled half-lives, you and I.*

THE MUMMY EXPERIMENT

The brain, it turns out, cannot be taken
through the nose with a hook
but must be drained through a small hole,
a deliberate crack in the skull
with the body hanging upside down to purge
the head impossibly of every last bit of its fluid.

Clean skin accepts death, clean
skin is also denial.
I rinse the mouth, stuff it with pure linen,
cover the face with resin.

I allow the eyes to sink
into their orbits, contemplate
glass additions under their lids,
eyeballs upon eyeballs, double vision.

One belly incision is never enough
to allow for adequate groping: the organs
are sliced and grabbed in chunks, half-careful
evisceration. The only other option
is to pull the whole
digestive tract down through itself.
Removal is its own reward.
The heart, this body's center, was meant to be left
where it lay, but accidents happen.
Knives are careless partners.

I wash the body's cavities with wine and herbs,
fill them with myrrh to keep it from stinking,
with natron-soaked packing to keep it from collapsing.
Forty days and forty nights: dehydration
requires salt and patience.
Natron, like being buried in the sand, requires trust
that mass is unimportant, that one-quarter
the original is adequate.

This body's—my body's, it belongs to me—teeth appear
out of proportion, uncontained.
When the skin is dark and snug, when it is not merely
leathery but leather itself,
I wash my body, repack it,
straighten it into
a proper position, something long and elegant, respectable.
I rub sacred oils into every crevice, each nearly incorruptible
epidermal cell. Juniper, cedar, cinnamon.
Wax in the nostrils, wax to close incisions.

Then begins the process of becoming
something recognizable again
by obscuring the detail of surfaces,
something with the appearance of mass and significance,
of space and gravity, like language. Wrapping is definition.
The mummy is formed. Now,
what will become of it?

Will this body be ground up as a cure-all taken as a tonic,
or thrown whole into the flames for a locomotive's fuel?
Perhaps it awaits a cocktail unwrapping:
guests snap photos as the lid is lifted, the form revealed
before dessert and brandy—they each pull a linen strip,
begin to unravel what I have taken such care to make.
My body's no treasure
found by slapdash grave robbers or determined curators.
It's not even a proper cadaver;
its preparedness is unteachable
and full of absent parts.

THE MANY WORLDS EXPERIMENT

Hypothesis:

I know the moment: his hold was gone. *Teneo,* I grasp.

The difference between up and down—either way, the fly by night, the
  inevitable.
And there's also the standing still, holding the railing, looking out over.

Beyond the shadow of my doubt: apologies, assurances, and the strange
  saplings.

When the sky is pregnant with snow, I can't tell good intentions from bad.
In the July heat, breath's a different weight and louder. I still can't tell.

Memory is measurable by fractional charges, particles charming us.

What could my mother and sister have been looking at
that they did not see his lips' last words?

Knowing the bottom urges the search for the top: an assumption of
  matter.

Who's to say the possibilities of any given day are as great
as its utter impossibilities? Is there an absolutely not? An absolutely all,
  branching wildly?

Oh dear, what can the matter be?

My lover buys a watch. Let's tell time a thing or two.
I have no proof of any given moment. Are you satisfied?

If he had lost his mind, as he did just that one night,
my mother could not have bucked up. She must have been beside herself.

It's not so much the fear of falling as the wanting to jump. And there's the
  quark to pay.

The physical is quantum mechanical. That's the premise: all relationships occur between the observer and the observed. Percentages are not options.

Methodology:

Within two weeks, the hair falls out all at once, what hasn't been already lost.

Despite what we know, some things take longer than the numbers would indicate:
    the drive to somewhere else (as opposed to the return home)
    your line at the grocery store (as opposed to the line you didn't choose)
    getting the story straight, revising until the words split, ambiguity
    the last minutes of any measured time (like waiting for the new year)
    processes watched closely (like the pot boiling, the dryer tumbling, trust emerging).

Motion sickness is in the head; eyes and ears have different versions of what's what.
Unless you have tumors in your abdomen. Then, all motion is sickness.

My lover tries ginger. My father bloats.

At the last moment, perhaps pain
because I held his hand so tightly, as if one sensation were as good as any other.

Trees falling, hands clapping. Who's to say where breath comes from?
Who's to say when words are just so?

Only sickness and love keep a person from leaving too quickly. *Go-go,* my first word.

Results:

The doctor knew it would be soon but didn't think *now*.
I knew, faraway, and could not swallow, rattled.

Water, water, everywhere, and not a drop to drink.

For every staving off, there is an equal and strange succumbing.
And the crackling. Like October leaves. And lungs filling.

Clickety-clacking. Pennies on tracks. Hand in hand, last words.

I threw my head back to see the sky, and his face centered in it.
Our smiles were upside-down to each other. He could not swim.

Previous possibilities slip away, but everything occurs at any next
   moment: *this* and *that*.

Here I am, fingering the absurdity of nature, delighting in her lack of
   common sense
and our need for it. Roll it around until top and bottom cannot be
   distinguished.

Swirling me in waves was the best he could do. It was more than
   enough charm for me.

Fear is the body's perception of altitude of one sort or another. One
   becomes the other.
Flight occurs when lift overcomes gravity, thrust overcomes drag.

I know when his body released him.

REGALIA, FROM THE LATIN *WORTHY OF A KING*

I've heard that in the mountains of South America,
men take revenge with a shot through the head
or ransack whole buses on the thin road,
laying victims out for public display,
cutting their throats to pull the tongue through,
splitting the sternum with a good knife
to get to the lungs and pull them out, too,
a necktie and a vest, an outfit for the dead
so that everyone knows *who* and *why*.
Here, too, we dress our dead,
sew their eyelids shut, their fingers together,
take their blood and stuff them.
If the wound is especially ugly,
we seal them up, close the caskets
as if we didn't want to see them again,
as if they had never ridden a bus down a thin road
or held our hands as we crossed the street.
We find our dead relatives in funeral parlors,
a pretty display of reeking flowers,
an altar telling us *look* and *look away*
as if we have no questions,
as if we can walk by with our heads bowed
and not look at who's leaving us behind,
as if we can separate moments from their causes,
stop in front of our fathers and say *good-bye.*

DETERIORATION, FROM THE LATIN *TO WEAR AWAY*

> *are you saying that iron understands*
> *time is another name for God?*
> "Rust," Lucille Clifton

Rust makes visible the power of oxygen—
pairs of atoms, breaths

not yet taken—on metal
which is supposed to be unyielding.

All distance weakens connections
when the stress outdoes the bond

and matter snaps at a certain pitch
like seams ripped with a seam ripper:

Staub Funeral Home, a space
exactly square with sharp edges, perfect

furniture, people in black clothes
that make position and speed impossible

to figure at once, skewing simultaneity
of interaction, ceremony, ritual,

a steady stream of hands against mine—
testing the limits of my outer shell's capacity

and valence—
of eyes observing my pauses, distractions,

my glances toward the body, my father,
his watchless wrist.

That's something I've kept: the watch.
It's time to move, allow force to overcome

inertia, air against my throat and suddenly
all of me spun from the cloud.

My sister will be the one who cries, bends
into my arms, a haphazard wrap

I piece together and, behind us,
the metal casket hemmed tight for burial,

against water, oxygen, and transformations.

RECURRING DREAM (2)

I did not visit the hospital yesterday. Or the day before. I know exactly what I was doing instead, what I ate, who spoke to me. I know the room by heart, the placement of the emesis basin, the possible and impossible angles of the bed. I understand the details, the smell from the tubes, the translucence of tape over skin. I have come to know his body's daily variations, a body's movement inward and outward. Yet I have forgotten, lost track of time. It has been twenty years. What will he think? I am dressing myself. My clothes are like bandages. Somewhere deep inside I know my father will not be there when I get to the hospital. I am caught, like a mummy, between worlds.

III. TOP/BOTTOM

A THEORY OF EVERYTHING

it is beautiful having
no disbelief to suspend.
   "THE SWIM," ROBIN BEHN

If there is God and if God counts,
   he counts failures, surely.

Not that my fingers couldn't form
   the chords on the neck

of the guitar, but that I cried
   in secret over performing for even

just one other person. *Youth*
   and *the girl in the blue dress*—me—

so different that you'd think
   I should have known the necessity of detail

all along. But I did know fathers
   die universally, with specificity

and narrative structure we cannot fail
   to notice as we strum

through our own plucky lives.
   If God adds things up, no wonder I fell

for a scientist, a failed pianist, a bibliophile.
   No wonder we all fall down: *kerplunk*

the only certain sound. The universe—everything—
   its resonance, from where I sit, like water,

takes only what it can
   from the numb sunlight.

INHABIT, FROM THE LATIN *TO HAVE AND HOLD*

after Audrey Hepburn as Holly Golightly

To have a little black dress and a cigarette holder
and no attachments. To name things for what they are
and wear slim ankle pants. Who wouldn't want
days and days with nothing to do but live
even if they came with a past one didn't always want
to forget? Who wouldn't want the chance, the song?
The writer upstairs is needy.

What does one really need? A Brazilian millionaire,
one might think. A ukulele, a shoplifted cat mask,
the fire escape with its landings just outside
the open windows.
Proximity is a safe distance.
A sheet of paper and an idea.

To carry off bangs and pretense
as if they were timeless. To exude happenstance.
But is it better to be the writer, to have distractions?

To pack my bags as if one place
is as good as another. There's no need to unpack every box.
There's no use thinking a taxi can take you far enough
or someone won't come after you
or you don't want him to.
Catch me in time, stop me. I have changed my outfit.
At some point, the rain begins like fingers tapping
on the window, like fingers on my keyboard.
Then, the past haunts me the way it should,
and I sit still and watch the someday that emerges.

STARSTRUCK

On a Saturday night, with love a thousand miles away
like stars to my naked eyes, I search the screen

for *Stella Dallas, The Lady Eve, It Happened One Night*—
Claudette Colbert's bared knee and, later,

the hanging sheet, her performance a witty constellation.
Gazing: these starlets at me—and me into the frames

that hold them like the night holds the space
station's predictable arc across my sky and his.

To find Katharine Hepburn, now that's something—
words pulsing, she swirls, lilts, stomps. Just when

she might spiral into regular orbit, transit the horizon,
she gathers herself into that swift, slick

magnitude, rises and spins. Is elegance beyond me
but innuendo now possible?

I lie there, silent, unable to move. Her throat burns with the smoke from her cigarette as she sucks the fire into her. He cuts off slices of my flesh with his pocket knife. The flesh is moist and glistening, richly colored and deep. It looks like pieces of liver you would buy at the grocery store. He is laughing, thinking. He feeds a slice to the woman. His fingers linger on her lips. They are giddy with it. She tilts her head back like a fat walrus. The flesh slips into their mouths like large oysters. My lover slurps the juices; the woman wipes blood from her chin. They devour me until they are full, almost sick with it. The air is smoky and filled with exuberant tête-à-tête.

RECURRING DREAM (4)

I open my mouth to speak, but the words are all wrong. They are black spiders falling from my lips. He is appalled. I stomp my feet. Our feet are like soldiers out of step. We cannot kill them fast enough. It looks as if we are dancing, as if our souls are happy and we cannot contain ourselves. He opens his mouth to speak, but the words are moths. They are dusty Lepidoptera unpinned from their mounting board, flying near the loud sun, searching for night. We swing our wild arms, batting their bodies. Their feet are sticky. Their wings make a spinning sound in our heads. We are dizzy with it and breathy like asthmatics. We wait to pass out, our mouths open and dry with exertion.

language like lightning, a state
                    of matter
ionized gas that does not behave
                    like itself
love in thunderstorms,
            the light large and quick
like the breathlessness of shock,
its collecting in the shoulders,

                    a form seen through red eyelids,
the blood vessels, bolts,
            another's fragile eyelids vulnerable
                            too, their countable creases,
                their blue undercast,
        blue jets: conelike and streaking upward
like a hand raised
                in the atmosphere
irises, secret capillaries, inward spirits arguing,
                ribbon: the wind blowing return strokes
                or swaying like hips

the wind a silent friction
            among millions of leaves,
                    the leaves themselves all sound,
—let the rain come.
                    Let the cool air maneuver over
        bodies in a mother's house,
        small above clouds: sprites
                the instant between
        one thought and many words
in a childhood
                bed—one misses
            light: less color, less heft
most what one cannot have.
Let there be light only
            if there is darkness—light

        is definition, separation, having
evidence, darkness
        is fluid movement, one thing
                into another because one cannot see
        otherwise, *revisions*

        elves: quick-dim glows
making light of
                        excitement and collision
and the bolt itself a fear.
                One misses thunderstorms, tongues
and teeth, the ability to breathe

        one's lungs to full capacity, the entire length
of a particular body
        illumination of the heavens
                        with the release of electricity
                as negative rolls over positive, positive
                over negative
        and the body's weightlessness is noticeable
weather, the want of looking through
                eyelids without the threat
        of seeing them

        or seeing them
burn away, disappearing
        into a phone call, into
gamma as a shriek, more intense power,
        something new,
discovered like the place where inner
                thigh meets torso, and warm, one imagines,
and dangerous
        the panicky night itself,
the swift-moving storm.

A FASCINATION: THE COLLEGE PARK AIRSHOW, 1992

for D.R.D.

Here, with the oil just burning off
in the hum of Pratt & Whitney engines, I imagine things:
the surviving Wright brother smiling, training

our first flyers, still awkward in uniforms.
Here, I climb into the cockpit of a Bell helicopter
with its blades curving wide just overhead,

the circles of instruments in front of me
as if I know where I might be going,
and my feet rest where men's feet have rested

for thirty years. Beyond them I can see the ground
and someone I know watching, his hand shading
his eyes to look at me inside

this thing. The engine is new—
the hull itself has been to Vietnam.
A body is used

until it reveals a structural flaw,
as when it hits the ground just so and the frame cracks.
Flyers, in 1911, determined how bombs could be dropped,

how machine guns might be fired from the sky.
Here, in the warm February of 1924, a helicopter
lifted with purpose

from this ground as if always possible,
as if it were only a matter of time
before anyone would consider

that if the rotor's center approaches the speed of sound,
the tips of the blade might exceed it, might rip the air—
it slaps back. Edges must be curved to fit the possible.

A woman a century ago thought it possible to prove
her husband's choice, be the first. Today, a man
dressed in red climbs atop a black and silver biplane,

stretches his arms out: he's a drop of blood in the sky,
a lunatic. Everyone waits for the fall, the line
that would save him. Long ago, the first plane of letters

moved paper through the air. No one knew
their words had left the earth, had made language a flight.
The man I know has started talking with a man bent

over a Boyd in a wooden shack where he has pried
six hundred screws from the sheet of one wing
and pulled back its corrugated skin

to expose its kitchen-plumbing fuel lines.
This hunched man thinks he can repair sixty years
of damage to hand-rolled aluminum: it matches no other.

This wing, its edge, is a discovered secret:
discard struts and run flaperons tip to belly
to create the power to move air with a hand and a stick.

This man leans over his table, drinks hot coffee
from a thermos and hands us pieces
of the airplane. We see why things don't fit.

The sky darkens as if something has seeped into it.
It is 1927: flyers learn to navigate with radio waves.
It is 1938: we walk among men in suspenders, the blimp

overhead as if bodies can buoy themselves unafraid,
as if my lover's promise to build is enough,
as if flight is the two of us rising in time.

COLLABORATION, FROM THE LATIN *TO SLIP TOGETHER*

with D.R.D.

Walking under and
out from under a pine tree,
with its thick leaf coats
netting three-inch flakes,
is like walking
through a curtain without opening it,
like seeing through the sky.
These flakes fall from grace, the friction
of six-sided bodies
sliding against
each other and against each other
and holding
in their long breathless drop
through the atmosphere.
Out in the open is to be
caught amidst, too,
and unable to see
the far-up beginnings.
Snow results from sublimation,
the skipping of a stage
in the process, the surprise
of its smallest particles
cohering suddenly at dew point.
This coalescence creates the inevitable,
increasing heft necessary
to move whole and growing
through the wet, rushing updraft.
Of kinds of snow,
which would I choose to be—pellet, plate,
capped column, spatial dendrite,
needle, star, irregular?
Just let me fall,
cold fists full against you.

While looking in an old Wheelock's Latin Grammar,
the recognition—a real rethinking—
that *inflect* means to bend, curve

like a burly blacksmith convincing iron,
to influence like a river persuading its banks.
Smidgen differences matter:

vacation = a retreat, vocation = a calling
like a god's prayer to you for a life,
vociferous like your ferocious needs

when you cast them, ironclad, toward me
with your stalwart voice.
In Latin, as in love, verbs reveal their subjects,

their true preoccupations, in endings:
there's where the man or woman lies,
where tense resides. To be passive is a form of *passion.*

Impinge: the deep blow. *Testimony:* a witness
grasps his balls and swears on them.
Collusion: together, the play, the pact, the blur.

We chart our own patient grammar,
infer logical connections, and *conversation* at last turns
our two bodies, back and forth together.

We attempt to decline, we struggle
with the absolute—ablative or otherwise—reach
for the subjunctive with all its wishful thinking:

O, were we to be brought under, utterly pinioned.
Silence, too, bends like fire and flood,
its tongue hot, wet, and cruelly desired.

CONTRACT, FROM THE LATIN *A DRAWING TOGETHER*

At first, your reasoning:
that lifelong monogamy is for the birds

with their quick hearts and flight.
Indeed, we might by now be twice divorced

or have a sad, unaltered life.
People assume one of two things:

you do not want to marry me
or you won't. People have told me so.

People say *husband* and I correct them
once or twice. They ask *why not?*

All girls draw pictures
of wedding gowns, learn bustles, think queens,

orchids, orange blossoms, organza.
Yes, yes, even me.

Later, perhaps even now, your thinking:
it's a game of chances, changes not worth making.

Sure, we might be left disappointed with each other
instead of merely with ourselves. A bird in the hand.

I see people rolling their eyes with *sin.*
They bite their lips as indictment works its logic.

Now, I can feel rebellious, unprotected, unreasonable,
enthused like a martyred saint.

I switch the stress from one syllable to the next:
a noun becomes a verb, the action begins.

I can't help myself, we all agree.
You have made another right decision,

avoided checkmate, rookery, thought things through.
We are not pawns, we think.

Nor birds—and yet, even we, luckily,
cannot cherish each other too much.

Or else, or else—yes, even me. Even you,
within reason, or else.

A RATIONAL CHOICE THEORY

Let's barter for love. Isn't a bargain better
than something we'd get for free?

Naturally, we select our reasoned preference
at any given moment. Later, we debate,

become churlish even. Can't the sensible
be sensual?

You give me your family history,
and I'll give you mine.

I offer efficiency, but it comes with
laundry day and multitasking.

You offer the one thing at a time, the reconciling
of a checkbook, the toothbrush to the grout,

but this comes with stacking
of books, bills, everything in view.

I am the out of sight but calendar stricken.
You wear the watch in this house. I keep time.

Exchange theories aren't good with details:
don't count your chickens,

this little piggie went to market, this little piggie had none.
We must think better than yesterday's wants

that we misguessed with good intentions.
Evolution's little luster favors us.

Let's barter every day: why notarize a trade-off,
why not question an even deal,

why not risk a less pecuniary life, bank something?
Love's expensive. Let's haggle.

AN EXPERIMENT OF VIOLENCE

Hypothesis:

A woman six years older than I
lives six blocks west of me.
She fails to notice, is given no notice
until her throat is cut
with her own kitchen knife.
Bloodletting should be done only to cure a life
from illness or sadness.

Test:

Don't live in a first-floor flat
or list your number in the phone book.
There are thirteen steps in a flight,
and seven digits is the limit of easy memory.
Stand up tall. Look ahead.
No, look around, know your surroundings.
Vary your route, your schedule.
Check the etymology: a leaf of paper,
perhaps to split or rend a day, a week, a month.
Do not fall, do not fall for someone.

Results:

On New Year's Day, I find a bullet
on the sidewalk. It is misshapen
from hitting the concrete at high velocity
from blocks away. The police had handed out
flyers asking that residents not fire
their guns in the air.
The celebration ricochets against my fingers.
I put the bullet in my pocket
to show you later.

RECURRING DREAM (5)

The falling, of course, the falling. And the finding
him there after all. He reads and hands me books,
one after the other. I notice their pages' folded
corners. The books overflow from my arms. I drop
them two and three at a time, and they disappear
past my feet liked buried coffins. I take out a pen,
more like a needle, it turns out, than a sword. I
suture my fingers together and can't type. He shows
me a nun bent over a manuscript. She paints tall
women gathering men like fish. She paints circles
like calendars. She snips my inky thread and, in her
awkward Latin, calls out: *Scribe. Ama. Haec eadem
sunt.* And the falling, the thread in the woman's hands,
my lover reading aloud.

THE STARS DON'T DANCE

The stars don't dance. I do. *Heel, toe. One-two-three.*
  I keep riddles like meteors. Look up, and, most often, you won't see

Those meteoric secrets for the clouds or the bright, distracting daylight.
  But on a clear, isolated night,

When a cold front lilts in, they leap across our sky, a curse
  Of pebbles let loose from the mouth of the universe.

Necessary dust, like percussion, they burn as soon as they hit the air,
  And we, awestruck by their brilliance, watch them inevitably dare

To quiet entirely in their quick, two-timing arcs. Count them: *one, two, three.*
  Search the ground, and you won't recognize what's left of them, of me

Strewn in cornfields, on rooftops, on shrinking glaciers
  Far from the three-quarter moment we now live. And yet here,

Secrets are still sloping behind cloud cover across our moony existence.
  The stars blankly stare. Meteors play the maddening music I dance.

WHAT THOUGHTS ARE WORTH

We all earn our thoughts by saving them,
by placing their coppery existences
on the rail that stretches to strange horizons.
We wait—patient—for the train. And then,

a shadow of a profile lingers
like the shape of a fountain, up slipping down.
We perceive the thumb's laudable charm
through the flat matter tingling our costly fingers.

Some collect in a blue bowl on a waist-high shelf
from the bottom of a pocket.
Others rest atop eyelids like memories
when the mind's inquiry mints itself.

The gaze remains, veritable. I slide
one on my lavish tongue, suckle and glide.

Quarks, first posited in the 1960s, have been verified by experiments to be the foundational constituents of matter. There are six types, or flavors, of quarks. *Up* and *down* are first-generation quarks; *charm* and *strange* are second generation; *top*, the most recently discovered quark, and *bottom* are third generation. Each quark has an electric charge that is a fraction of the standard charge so that, for instance, a proton consists of two up quarks and a down quark for a standard charge of one. A single quark does not occur alone.

MOMENTS, CAUSES
The quotation by Henri Poincaré is from Leonard Schlain's *Art & Physics: Parellel Visions in Space, Time & Light.*

THEORIES OF HANDWRITING
Debate exists as to whether Mandarin is a dialect or a language. Here, Mandarin is used to distinguish traditional from simplified Chinese. The latter refers to the standardization and simplification of written Chinese by the People's Republic of China to promote literacy. Thanks to Arthur Sze and Celia Tinyan Ko for additional insights.

A THEORY OF PALMS
Hypergraphia is "the medical term for an overpowering desire to write," which Alice W. Flaherty explores in her book *Midnight Disease: The Drive to Write, Writer's Block, and the Creative Brain.*

NOTES ON A FEW ATOMIC SCIENTISTS
The quotation from Marie Curie is the last stanza of an occasional poem included in Susan Quinn's *Marie Curie: A Life.*

A GAME THEORY
Game theory is an applied mathematical theory used to understand individuals' choices, particularly their economic choices, in relation to maximizing their returns. Game theory has also been used to analyze military strategy, ethics, and natural selection.

Constituents of Matter

All planets in the solar system orbit counterclockwise if one were to look from the north pole of the sun, and most rotate counterclockwise as well. Venus has retrograde, or clockwise, rotation. *Eccentricity* is a measure of an orbit's deviation from a circle; Venus's orbit exhibits little eccentricity, whereas Earth has a more elliptical orbit.

Ontogeny recapitulates phylogeny was a theory in biology posited by a contemporary of Charles Darwin to explain humans' resemblance to animals by linking ontogeny—the embryonic development of a given species—to phylogeny—the evolutionary history of that species.

The Many Worlds Experiment

The many worlds interpretation of quantum mechanics proposes parallel universes continually splitting off into different states so that all possibilities exist at every juncture, though the observer inhabits only one universe in one state at any given time.

A Theory of Everything

A theory of everything is the sought-after unification of theories that would use a single mathematical framework to explain all physical phenomena, from quarks to planets.

A Rational Choice Theory

Rational choice theory is largely an economic theory used to understand and predict how individuals—and entities like nations and corporations, which are presumed to act with human reason—weigh a variety of options and preferences in decision making.

Recurring Dream (5)

The nun refers to Saint Hildegard of Bingen.